GECKOS

LIVING WILD

Published by Creative Education
P.O. Box 227, Mankato, Minnesota 56002
Creative Education is an imprint of The Creative Company
www.thecreativecompany.us

Design and production by Mary Herrmann
Art direction by Rita Marshall
Printed in the United States of America

Photographs by Alamy (Arco Images GmbH, Everett Collection Inc., Jeff Greenberg, John Insull), Dreamstime (Yuriy Chaban, Isselee, Mgkuijpers, Pebat, Roughcollie, Chris Turner), Getty Images (James Gerholdt, HNH Images, Michael Leach, Jim Merli), iStockphoto (ankh-fire, Neutronman), Newscom (L. LEE GRISMER/AFP), Shutterstock (bierchen, Steve Bower, Melissa Brandes, Papa Bravo, George Burba, DDCoral, Natali Glado, Ralf Gosch, Cathy Keifer, Peter Krejzl, David Lee, Nikonboy, Dean Pennala, Dr. Morley Read, Fedor Selivanov, smishonja, watcharakun), SuperStock (Minden Pictures, Tips Images), Wikipedia (Rémi Bigonneau, Central Bank of Russia, Brian Gratwicke, Hinrich Kaiser, Alfeus Liman, Psumuseum, Mickey Samuni-Blank, Vassil, Erik Zobrist/NOAA Restoration Center, Zug and Fisher)

Library of Congress Cataloging-in-Publication Data
Gish, Melissa.
Geckos / Melissa Gish.
p. cm. — (Living wild)
Includes bibliographical references and index.
Summary: A scientific look at geckos, including their habitats, physical characteristics such as their tuberculate skin, behaviors, relationships with humans, and variety of the vocalizing lizards in the world today.
ISBN 978-1-60818-417-0
1. Geckos—Juvenile literature. I. Title. II. Series: Living wild.

QL666.L245G57 2014
597.95'2—dc23   2013031812

CCSS: RI.5.1, 2, 3, 8; RST.6-8.1, 2, 5, 6, 8; RH.6-8.3, 4, 5, 6, 7, 8

9 8 7 6 5 4 3 2

ℭ CREATIVE EDUCATION

GECKOS

Melissa Gish

In the small town of Puako, Hawaii, light rain begins to fall. . . . A gecko emerges from its daytime

hiding place among the rocks of a flower garden and climbs up the side of a house.

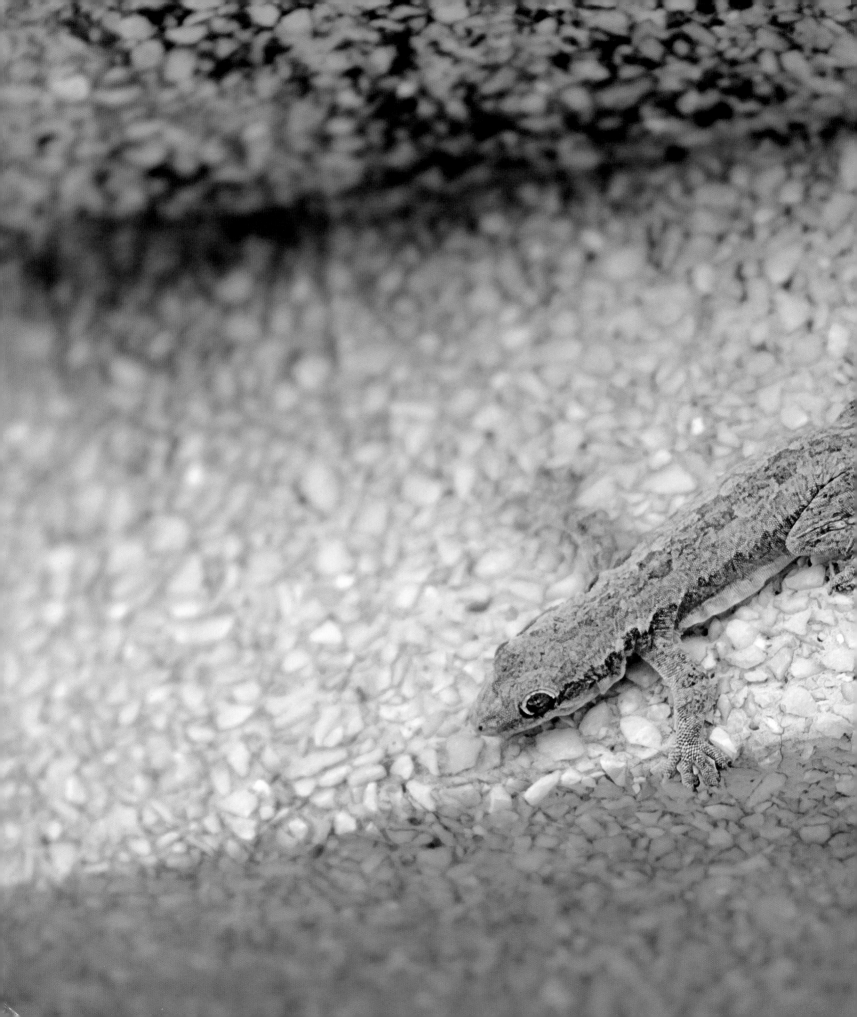

In the small town of Puako, Hawaii, light rain begins to fall as the sun dips below the horizon. A fox gecko emerges from its daytime hiding place among the rocks of a flower garden and climbs up the side of a house. It sits on the ledge of an open window, licking moisture off its nose and bulging eyes. A kowhai moth flutters past the gecko's head, drawing its attention. The gecko follows the moth into the house and races up the wall, navigating around a clock and several pictures. The moth bounces erratically around a light fixture on the ceiling. The gecko scurries across the ceiling, its eyes transfixed on the moth's movements, until it comes to a sudden stop. The moment the moth settles to rest, the gecko leaps on the hapless creature, swallowing it whole. Then the gecko continues on its nightly patrol of the kitchen.

WHERE IN THE WORLD THEY LIVE

■ **New Caledonian Giant Gecko**
New Caledonia and neighboring islands

■ **Leopard Gecko**
Asian deserts, Pakistan, India

■ **Tokay Gecko**
from India throughout Southeast Asia

■ **Madagascar Day Gecko**
Madagascar

■ **Middle Eastern Short-fingered Gecko**
Middle East

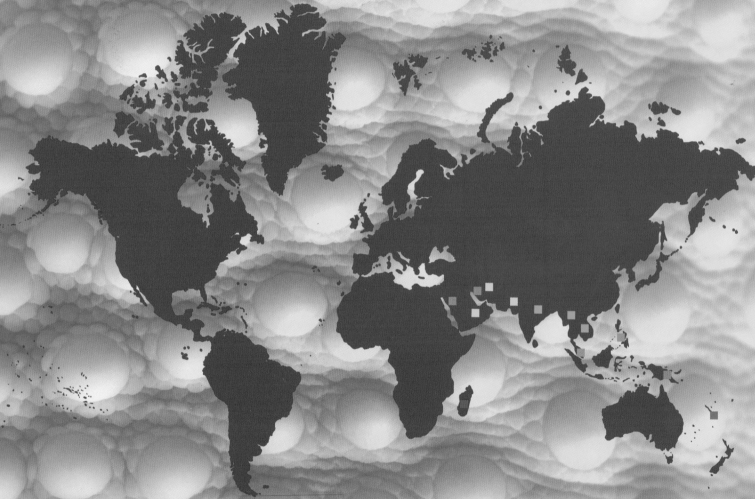

Nearly 1,000 gecko species have been found, with new ones surprising scientists in remote locales around the globe. The largest of the five subfamilies, Gekkoninae, contains more than 850 of the species, many of which live throughout Asia and Africa. The colored dots on this page represent native origins of seven unique gecko species.

■ **Mourning Gecko**
Southeast Asian islands

■ **Bumblebee Gecko**
Manus Island of Papua New Guinea

CLIMBERS AND GLIDERS

As the only lizards that can vocalize, geckos may have provided their own name. The word "gecko" may have come from the Malaysian *gekoq*, which refers to the Tokay gecko's barking sound. Like most reptiles on the planet, geckos have remained mostly unchanged for the past 100 million years. Of the roughly 5,800 lizard species on Earth, more than 950 are members of the family Gekkonidae, or geckos, which can be further divided into 5 subfamilies, as based on physical characteristics and geographic location. Geckos are the only lizards capable of vocalizations (other than hissing), making chirping or even screaming sounds. Some species are found around the planet, while others are limited to only Old World or New World locations. All geckos are carnivorous, meaning they eat other animals, but colors, skin textures, and sizes vary greatly among the species.

The world's smallest gecko, Jaragua Sphaero (named for Grupo Jaragua, the organization that secured protected habitat for this species in the Dominican Republic), is 0.6 inch (1.5 cm) long and can sit comfortably on a quarter. The world's largest gecko, the two-foot-long (61 cm)

Web-footed geckos have webs of skin between their toes that help them skitter across Africa's Namib Desert.

The cat gecko of Southeast Asia is named for its feline habit of curling its tail around its body and head to sleep.

Kawekaweau, was driven to **extinction** in New Zealand by rats and ermines that traveled with the Europeans who **colonized** the islands in the late 1800s. The record is now held by the New Caledonian giant gecko, which is around 14 inches (35.6 cm) long. This gecko is found on the island of New Caledonia, located about 750 miles (1,207 km) east of Australia, and on several small neighboring islands.

Geckos generally rely on **camouflage** as protection from predators. Geckos found in rocky, desert habitats, such as the Middle Eastern short-fingered gecko, are typically tan or yellow in color with dark splotches or bands that help them blend in with sand and rocks. Geckos found in rainforest habitats, such as New Zealand's common green gecko and the Madagascar day gecko, may be bright green to match the color of leaves in the forest. Some geckos also have colorful markings that reflect light. Australia's northern leaf-tailed gecko hides from predators by sharing the rough texture and dull colors of tree bark and dead leaves.

If camouflage doesn't work, a gecko may resort to its second line of defense: caudal autonomy, or tail loss. When captured by a predator, a gecko can contract the muscles in its tail so tightly that a part of its tail breaks off. The broken

Camouflage is a gecko's best
defense against birds, tree-
dwelling rodents, and its
greatest predator—snakes.

When a gecko drops its tail, the blood vessels around the break tighten to prevent excessive blood loss.

appendage will continue to twitch for some time, which is meant to distract the predator while the gecko escapes. Some species, such as the crested gecko, will remain tailless for the rest of their lives, but most species can regrow a broken tail within two to eight weeks. However, the new tail may not be the same color or shape as the original. Like all lizards, geckos lack external ears. Instead, a flap of skin called a tympanic membrane covers the ear openings on the sides of the head.

Because geckos are reptiles, they are ectothermic animals, which means that their bodies depend on external sources of heat, and their temperatures change with the environment. Some geckos are diurnal, or active during the day. In the morning and late afternoon, these geckos lie in sunny places to warm their bodies. At midday, when the sun becomes stronger, they retreat to the shade of trees or rocks to prevent overheating. Most geckos are nocturnal, which means they rest or sleep during the day and become active at night. Nocturnal geckos have slitted pupils (like cats) and can open their eyes wide to see better in dim light. Diurnal geckos have round pupils, like humans, which can adjust to see better in daylight.

The frog-eyed gecko, found in the deserts of Central Asia, has loose scales that it can shake to mimic a rattlesnake.

A gecko's tongue cleans its eyes and identifies objects through scents rubbed on the roof of the mouth.

Nearly all lizards have moveable eyelids and can blink, but only a handful of gecko species have this ability. Most geckos do not blink and have clear scales, called brilles, covering their eyes. They clean these eye coverings by frequently licking them. Only the 18 gecko species making up the family Eublepharidae, or eyelid geckos, can blink using moveable eyelids. The leopard gecko, which is a popular pet, is an eyelid gecko.

Geckos have soft skin covered with small bumps called tubercles instead of the dry, scaly skin typical of other lizards. Some geckos are like other lizards in that they climb by clutching rough surfaces with their clawed feet, but most gecko species have specialized toe pads called adhesive lamellae that allow them to climb straight up and walk upside down on smooth surfaces—even glass. The gecko has five widespread toes on each foot. The bottom surface of each toe is made up of flaps of skin that are covered with tiny hairs called setae—each hair 10 times slenderer than a human hair. More than 1.6 million setae cover each foot.

Because the hairs are so small, the **molecules** of each seta touch the molecules of the gecko's climbing surface.

Leopard geckos can live for 20 years, are easy to feed, and do not need much space, making them good pets.

In the moist rainforest, flying geckos often dig under the soft, decaying bark of dead trees to hunt for insects.

When molecules come into such contact, they become attracted to each other by a power called van der Waals force (named for a Dutch **physicist**). In essence, geckos' toes and the surfaces they touch are like two magnets sticking to each other. Not all gecko species have this ability, but for those that do, the van der Waals force is so powerful that pulling a gecko free of a surface requires a feat of strength. Geckos with super climbing ability will fall from most surfaces only if they let go, and to let go, geckos must bend their toes backward to release the setae a row at a time. They are able to do this with such incredible speed that the movement is virtually invisible to the naked eye.

Six species of gecko are known as flying geckos, or parachute geckos. These geckos have thin flaps of skin on their underbellies between their limbs and along their necks that expand like parachutes when the gecko leaps off a surface into the air. These **membranes** allow the gecko to glide and even maneuver through the air. Flying geckos, which are found only in Southeast Asia, can glide as far as 200 feet (61 m) before making an upward swooping motion that allows them to land softly on a surface.

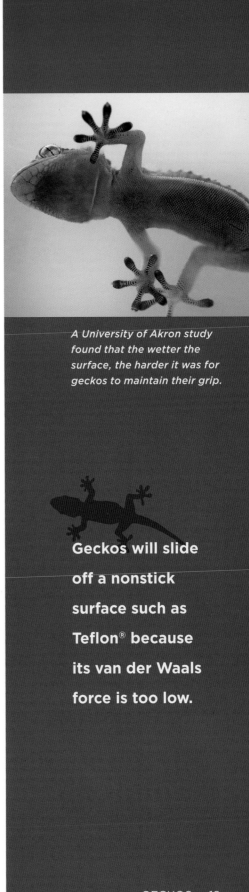

A University of Akron study found that the wetter the surface, the harder it was for geckos to maintain their grip.

Geckos will slide off a nonstick surface such as Teflon® because its van der Waals force is too low.

While waiting for its tail to regrow, a gecko can be vulnerable to attacks from which it cannot escape.

SCREAMING REPTILES

I n the wild, geckos face many dangers, from birds and snakes that prey on them to humans who collect them—sometimes illegally—for the pet and traditional Asian medicine trades. As both predators and prey, geckos live their lives in constant peril. If they can survive the first year, they will be old enough to reproduce. Geckos have no specific season for reproduction; rather, changes in temperature, rainfall, and amount of sunlight trigger and influence a gecko's readiness to produce offspring.

Like all lizards, the various gecko species reproduce in a number of ways. Some geckos, such as the Southern Hemisphere's mourning gecko, are able to reproduce parthenogenetically. This means females can have offspring without mating with males. Such reproduction is possible because these geckos are born with all the **genetic** material needed to produce clones, or living copies, of themselves. All geckos of a parthenogenetic species are female. Other gecko species, such as leopard and crested geckos, require a male and a female to reproduce. The majority of gecko species prefer to live alone. When they want to mate, they

Although geckos have no medical value, some people in China and Southeast Asia believe they can cure serious diseases.

In the wild, males fight over females, but captive geckos also fight over territory and food—sometimes to the death.

Cochran's croaking gecko never touches the ground, living only in the ficus and palm trees of its Caribbean habitat.

must find each other first, and they often have to travel over expanses that can be great in relation to a gecko's size.

Like most lizards, geckos have tiny holes on the insides of their upper thighs called femoral pores. In females, these pores are barely visible, but in males, the pores are larger and bumpy. Glands in the gecko's body produce scents called pheromones, which are secreted from the femoral pores. When a female has eggs inside her body that are ready to be fertilized, her pheromones will indicate that she is ready to mate, and male geckos will be attracted to her. Males may bite and wrestle with each other—even to the death—over the right to mate with a female. After mating, a process that can take from 10 seconds to 10 minutes, the male leaves the female on her own to produce 1 or 2 offspring.

The way baby geckos develop varies by species. All the geckos found on the island of New Zealand and some on New Caledonia are ovoviviparous (*OH-voh-vy-VIP-er-us*). This means the females produce soft, flexible eggs that are held within the body while the **embryos** inside the eggs develop. The fully formed young hatch out of the eggs and then emerge from their mother's body. Other geckos are oviparous (*oh-VIP-er-us*), which means they

select a nest site and lay eggs like birds do. Depending on the species, the gecko's eggs may be tough and leathery or hard like a chicken egg.

Oviparous geckos lay one or two eggs in a protected area that is damp, such as a hole in a tree or beneath bark or a rock. A mother may stand guard over the eggs, which, depending on the species, take six to eight weeks to hatch. Geckos in tropical climates may lay eggs several times throughout the year, while geckos in cooler climates may reproduce just once per year.

Regardless of how they developed, once baby geckos arrive, mother geckos have nothing more to do with

A leopard gecko lays eggs in pairs 5 or 6 times per year; the eggs hatch 40 to 60 days after they are laid.

From the moment they hatch, baby geckos have the same climbing and clinging abilities as adults.

them. Newly hatched geckos must rely on camouflage and stillness to avoid predators or simply run away when they can. However, even the speediest baby gecko is often no match for a spider, snake, or larger lizard, and caudal autonomy is often not useful when the entire gecko is small enough to nab with one bite. Some geckos utilize additional defenses. Found only on New Caledonia, the Bavay's gecko defends itself by secreting a smelly oil similar to how a skunk sprays musk.

Once a gecko matures and establishes regular feeding and resting areas, it may defend its territory from invaders who get too close, vocalizing with chirps or screams. Geckos also make sounds by clicking or vibrating the tongue against the roof of the mouth. In addition, geckos may exhibit behaviors called posturing. Males are particularly hostile toward each other when seeking mates. A defensive gecko will stand stiffly, bob its head, and wag or vibrate its tail. A gecko may also step sideways toward an intruder to ward it off. Females guarding eggs also exhibit posturing and vocalization, and captive geckos have even been observed posturing and screaming when their keepers reached into their enclosures. Even very young geckos are able to scream loudly when disturbed.

Geckos are either ground-dwelling or arboreal reptiles, meaning they hunt for food on the ground or in the trees. Depending on their habitat, small ground-dwelling geckos search under leaf litter, rocks, and tree roots for a variety of prey including crickets, worms, beetles, and spiders. Small arboreal geckos typically hunt caterpillars, moths, flies, and spiders. Large geckos can be formidable predators. While the New Caledonian giant gecko eats fruit, it also hunts other lizards, and despite geckos' having no teeth, the Tokay gecko—the world's second-largest gecko species—

Because of their ability to communicate, geckos are considered to be the most vocal of all lizards.

The two-inch (5 cm) Peringuey's leaf-toed gecko was believed extinct until it was found in South African marshes in 1992.

Madagascar day geckos use their leafy-green-colored camouflage to sneak up on insect prey.

easily crushes the hard shells of the beetles on which it feeds. Some of the world's largest geckos—those up to 14 inches (35.6 cm) long—live and hunt in the tropics of Southeast Asia and Oceania (the term for all the islands throughout the tropical Pacific from Australia to Hawaii). Kandyan and bark geckos hunt small snakes, and bridled bent-toed geckos prey on small birds and rodents.

Captive geckos typically cannot have a diet as varied as that of wild geckos, and captive geckos can suffer from diseases and **parasites** if they are not fed properly. Crickets, mealworms, wax worms, and even pinky mice (baby mice only a few days old) typically make up a captive gecko's diet. To provide a gecko with optimal nutrition, keepers often feed the insects and worms vitamin- and mineral-enriched food right before the prey become meals themselves. This practice is called gut-loading. Wild geckos typically survive no more than 3 to 6 years, but in captivity, many gecko species that are kept healthy often live for 15 to more than 20 years. A leopard gecko owned by Ron Tremper, a former reptile specialist at the Fresno Zoo in California, was more than 30 years old as of 2013—the oldest gecko on record.

The Tokay gecko can change its spots from brown when in dark surroundings to red when in light surroundings.

THE GECKO

The Gecko lying on his stone
Is always very much alone,
Nor is the reason hard to trace
By those who've seen its form and face
It's hard to realise a mite
Can be so venomous a sight,
Or in its little frame compress
Such concentrated ugliness.
No wonder other creatures fly
Each time a Gecko ambles by.
No wonder that its chosen mate
Recoils from the connubial state.
Yet underneath its skin, we're told,

There beats a heart of purest gold.
Its children do not know neglect;
It treats its mother with respect.
It never, ever beats its wife,
And lives a most unblemished life.
Its aspect is its sole defence
Against the world's malevolence.
So when you see a Gecko stay
Uncharitable thoughts and say:—
"The gruesome are not always gross—
even a reptile bears its cross!"

by Leon Gellert (1892-1977)

GOOD LUCK GECKOS

G eckos are considered good luck charms in some **cultures** and bad luck in others. In northern India, one traditional belief holds that if a gecko falls or jumps on a person, that person will become ill. In southern India, however, the gecko is honored. There it is believed that a person who touches a golden gecko will receive *moksha*, or peace. Because geckos are difficult to catch, a number of temples in India house statues of golden geckos that people can touch. People who believe good luck can come from geckos often visit the Varadaraja Temple in the state of Tamil Nadu in southern India. In this temple, gold and silver gecko statues adorn the ceiling and can be touched for good luck if visitors can reach them.

The gecko's mysterious climbing ability has inspired the **mythology** and legends of people around the world, but nowhere are geckos more prevalent than in Hawaiian culture. Many Hawaiian tribes worshiped geckos as *aumakua*, or family gods. These people believed that some of their ancestors took the form of geckos after death and would provide protection and wisdom to the person who dreamed about them. One of the aumakua, named Mo'o,

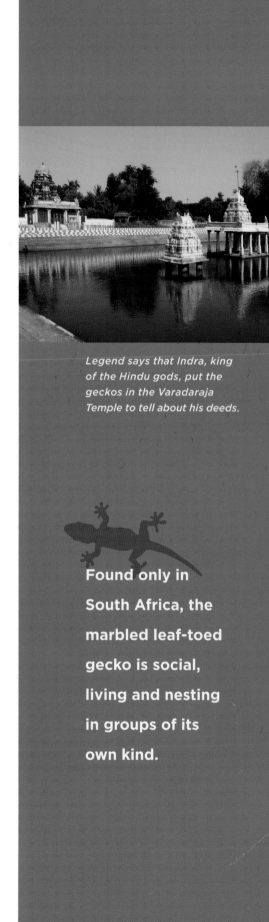

Legend says that Indra, king of the Hindu gods, put the geckos in the Varadaraja Temple to tell about his deeds.

Found only in South Africa, the marbled leaf-toed gecko is social, living and nesting in groups of its own kind.

Besides geckos, the Indian Ocean island of Mauritius was once home to flightless birds such as the dodo.

Geckos can reach vertical speeds of 40 inches (102 cm) per second— equivalent to a human running 81 miles (130 km) per hour up a wall.

was the offspring of Father Sky and Mother Earth. Mo'o is depicted in stories as an enormous black flying reptile that inhabits caves and visits fishponds.

Although Mo'o appears to be fearsome, this helpful goddess brought fish to the fishponds and often took on the form of a small gecko to visit humans without frightening them. As a gecko, Mo'o would visit homes and watch over the people. She was also the mother of other powerful beings in Hawaiian mythology, including Namakaokaha'i, ruler of the oceans; Pele, goddess of volcanoes; the Hi'iaka sisters, who made helpful herbs grow; and Kapo'ulakina'u, the goddess of the dead.

In Hawaiian tradition, the gecko's body is the symbol of the connection that humans maintain with their ancestors. The gecko's eyes represent the generations to come. The front feet are the children; the upper body is the parents; and the lower body is the grandparents and elder family members. The gecko's flexible spine, connecting all the body parts, represents the ancestors, while the tail is the family's guardian spirit. Many Hawaiians still believe that welcoming a gecko into one's home brings good luck, while killing a gecko brings bad luck. Despite their

traditional beliefs, most residents of the Hawaiian Islands recognize the gecko's usefulness in controlling insect pests and eagerly accept these creatures into their homes.

With their bright colors and unique patterns, geckos have been popular images on the postage stamps of many nations. Mauritius released a 1978 stamp with ornate day and orange-spotted day geckos, and a 1998 set featuring Round Island day, Durrell's night, Rodrigues day (now

Madagascar's gold dust day gecko has been introduced to Hawaii and other Pacific islands, where it now flourishes.

The turnip-tailed gecko, found from Mexico to Brazil, is named for its enlarged tail, which it uses to store fat.

extinct), and lesser night geckos. A 1993 stamp from Cambodia features the Kuhl's flying gecko, and two 1994 stamps from Tajikistan feature the even-fingered and frog-eyed geckos. Four gecko species native to Fiji appear on a set of 2003 stamps in that country, and the Federated States of Micronesia included the leopard gecko in its 2004 set of reptiles and amphibians. Palau's 2010 "Reptiles of the World" stamp set includes the common house gecko and the Indo-Pacific tree gecko, and Grenada's 2011 "Reptiles of the Caribbean" stamp series includes the tropical house gecko. The house, fantastic,

Vincent's least, and turnip-tailed geckos appear as part of a 2011 stamp set from Dominica as well.

Geckos are found on coins the world over, too. The stump-tailed gecko is featured on the 1979 five-cent coin from the Republic of Kiribati. The Turkmenistan eyelid gecko appeared on the Russian 50-ruble coin in 1993 and 1-ruble coin in 1996. Also in 1996, this gecko appeared on the Turkmenistan 500 manat as part of an endangered animals coin series. The ring-tailed gecko, one of Australia's largest geckos, appears on the Cook Islands' 1998 one-dollar coin.

American writer Bruce Hale, who began writing when he lived in Tokyo, created two of children's literature's most interesting gecko characters: Chet and Moki, who, according to Hale's website, are second cousins. In the Chet Gecko Mysteries series, the title character is a witty fourth-grade detective from Emerson Hicky Elementary. In the 15-book series, which began in 2000, Chet tracks down school vandals, thieves, kidnappers, and hypnotists who make sleepy zombies of his classmates. In the Moki books, the title character is a Hawaiian surfing gecko who just likes to have fun. The first book in the series, *The*

The stump-tailed gecko, featured on two coins from the Republic of Kiribati, is also known as the sugar lizard.

The four Ninja Turtles returned to TV in animated form in the 2000s and were featured in a 2007 movie.

Only three specimens of zigzag velvet geckos have been found since the species was discovered in Australia in 2002.

Legend of the Laughing Gecko (1989), explains why geckos are considered good luck in Hawaii. In Moki and the Magic Surfboard (1996), Moki travels through time, and in Moki the Gecko's Best Christmas Ever (1998), Moki saves Santa after his sleigh has a mishap over the ocean.

On television in the mid-1980s, Teenage Mutant Ninja Turtles became a popular animated show that spawned a series of comic books. One of the turtles' adversaries was Mondo Gecko, a gecko exposed to the same green ooze that mutated the turtles. Mondo Gecko was raised by the evil Mr. X, who turned Mondo into a criminal. After some fierce fighting, the Ninja Turtles convince Mondo to change his ways, and Mondo moves into the sewers near the turtles, where he becomes a friendly neighbor. In 1994, Gex the Gecko was introduced in the video game Gex, which was followed by Gex: Enter the Gecko in 1998 and Gex 3: Deep Cover Gecko in 1999, which became the best-selling adventure game for PlayStation that year.

Perhaps the most recognizable gecko on television is the GEICO gecko, the animated spokesperson for the GEICO insurance company. Simply named "The Gecko," the Madagascar day gecko with a British accent

first appeared in a TV commercial in 1999, where he asked viewers to stop calling him, explaining that he was a gecko and not GEICO. The Gecko became popular, and GEICO credited him with increasing their sales. Two years later, The Gecko was adopted as the mascot of GEICO and became part of the company's official logo. Since then, The Gecko has starred in many more television commercials, and GEICO partnered with the Association of Zoos and Aquariums to sponsor a traveling exhibit on geckos—including special appearances by The Gecko—that ran from 2008 to 2010.

Inflatable likenesses of The Gecko appear in parades, and the popular mascot released a book, You're Only Human, *in 2013.*

While many gecko species prefer moist habitats, geckos cannot swim and may drown if they get stuck in puddles or pools.

UNCOVERING GECKO SECRETS

The psychedelic gecko was among the 208 species of wildlife discovered in Vietnam's Greater Mekong region in 2010.

New gecko species are discovered regularly—and mostly by accident. In July 2008, a research team led by Dr. Steve Richards of the South Australia Museum conducted a general wildlife survey in the Kaijende Highlands of central Papua New Guinea. Richards's team documented a sighting of a previously unknown gecko species that was soon categorized as a bent-toed gecko—with claws instead of toe pads. In 2010, on Papua New Guinea's Manus Island, biologists with the United States Geological Survey and the Papua New Guinea National Museum discovered a black-and-gold-striped gecko, which they dubbed the bumblebee gecko. Genetic test results from the four specimens recovered from the island show that this species most likely exists only on Manus Island.

In 2010, a purple gecko with a yellow head and orange limbs was discovered on Hon Khoai Island in Vietnam. Researchers nicknamed it the psychedelic gecko. As recently as 2012, a single specimen of a previously unknown species of bent-toed gecko was found on East Montalivet Island off the northwestern coast of Australia. Researchers noted

Island animals, such as the Monito gecko, often suffer greatly from the introduction of invasive species.

The pictus gecko of Madagascar is also called the ocelot gecko for its spotted skin pattern, resembling the small nocturnal jungle cats.

some important distinctions about it. The **gravid** female gecko was less than five inches (12.7 cm) long, which is much smaller than most other bent-toed geckos, and while other bent-toed geckos normally carry two eggs, this gecko carried only a single egg inside her body.

Many gecko populations, such as those of the Mediterranean house gecko, are strong. That species was introduced into Florida in 1910 and has since spread its reach into neighboring states as well. However, other gecko populations are declining, and conservationists fear that unknown gecko species could become extinct before they are even discovered. Many geckos are endemic to islands around the world, which means they are native to those islands and found nowhere else. The greatest threat to endemic geckos is the introduction of nonnative species into the **ecosystem**, which may cause geckos to not only contend with new predators but also force them to compete for food with other—sometimes larger or more aggressive—species.

The Monito gecko is found only on Puerto Rico's Monito Island. This gecko has been listed as endangered on the Red List of Threatened Species that is published annually by the International Union for Conservation of

Nature (IUCN), and in 1982, the U.S. Fish & Wildlife Service placed the Monito gecko on the Endangered Species List. The Monito's population has likely been in persistent decline since the mid-20th century, when rats were introduced onto the human-free island. Conservationists have tried to eliminate the rats and regularly monitor the geckos since they were discovered in the 1970s, but fewer than 250 of these reptiles remain on Monito Island. Also listed as endangered on the U.S. Endangered Species List are two species of day gecko, and the Serpent Island gecko is classified as threatened.

The Mediterranean house gecko, also called the Turkish gecko, is a nocturnal hunter of moths and beetles.

All gecko species native to New Zealand give birth to live young—usually twins—rather than lay eggs.

Conservation plans for geckos are basically nonexistent in most parts of the world simply because geckos are difficult to find in the wild. More often, researchers study geckos in controlled laboratory settings to find out how native geckos compete for food in a habitat with nonnative geckos or how the effects of climate change (such as changes in humidity, sunlight, and temperature) influence certain gecko species. However, one research project being conducted in New Zealand is as unique as the rare geckos that serve as its subject.

New Zealand comprises two large islands, called North Island and South Island, as well as many small islands. South Island is home to a variety of geckos that survive seasonal temperature shifts, from rainy summers to snowy winters. Collectively called alpine geckos, these nocturnal reptiles are helping researchers uncover some of the secrets of gecko life. Biologist Mandy Tocher began her career studying tropical frogs, but in 2004, she was selected to lead an alpine gecko research project directed by New Zealand's Department of Conservation and funded by the major clothing company Kathmandu. What made Tocher's project so unusual was the fact that two of her research partners were a dog named Putiputi rapua and a gecko named Gerald. Using Gerald the gecko as a teaching aid, Tocher trained Putiputi rapua to sniff out geckos and to lie down when she found one. This allowed Tocher and her team to locate nocturnal geckos in dense leaf litter—a task that previously had been impossible. A second dog was later added to the project, which yielded much useful information.

To help conserve geckos, many governments are working to eliminate invasive species such as rats from uninhabited islands where geckos once roamed in relative safety. Rats were finally eliminated from Matiu/Somes Island, which

Harlequin geckos have one or two offspring every three to five years, making them difficult to conserve.

In 2006, French researchers recovered eggs from an island in the South Pacific and hatched *Lepidodactylus buleli*, a new gecko species.

The Wellington green gecko has yellow soles, and the blue flesh lining its mouth is visible when it barks.

When startled or disturbed, Madagascar's satanic leaf-tailed gecko (opposite) opens its bright red mouth to show aggression.

lies between New Zealand's North and South Islands, in the 1980s, and in 2007, conservationists reintroduced a pair of Wellington green geckos to the island. Before releasing them, however, scientists attached radio transmitters to the geckos' small bodies. The tiny electronic devices were held in place by soft fabric tape and sent signals that the scientists used to track the geckos' locations on the island. The information was useful in helping conservationists safely release 30 more Wellington green geckos on Matiu/Somes Island over the next two years.

Geckos are also helping scientists improve human life. Evolutionary ecologist and **morphologist** Duncan Irschick of the University of Massachusetts studies the way geckos climb. His work has led to the recent understanding of how geckos exhibit van der Waals force and suggested ways technology could be developed to artificially mimic gecko movement. Irschick's research may someday lead to the construction of gloves and boots that use van der Waals force in much the same way that geckos' toe pads do.

Not only do many gecko species around the world suffer from habitat loss and predation from introduced species, many are under pressure from the exotic pet

trade as well. Responsible gecko fanciers purchase only **captive-bred** specimens, but too often people buy wild-caught geckos, which can destroy populations. Innovative research methods to study elusive geckos are needed to uncover the secrets of these fascinating reptiles and conserve them for generations to come.

Only seven zoos in the U.S. keep satanic leaf-tailed geckos, and the San Diego Zoo breeds these reptiles.

ANIMAL TALE: THE TOKAY GECKO AND HIS BRIDE

In Southeast Asia, geckos are common in rural villages, where many people consider them good luck symbols. The Bru people of northern Vietnam have a rich tradition of myths about the animals found on their coffee plantations—particularly geckos, whose name in their language is Toc Ke (*TOE-kay*). This story tells how the Tokay gecko of Vietnam came to be.

Long ago, there lived a green lizard name Toc Ke. He was a magical lizard, but he was lonely. One day, as he was drinking water from a stream, he saw a beautiful girl on the opposite bank. He watched her and fell in love. As she bent to dip a bucket into the stream, her foot slipped on a rock, and she tumbled into the water. Toc Ke dove in to rescue her, pulling her up onto the bank. Before the girl could open her eyes, Toc Ke transformed himself into a handsome man.

At night, Toc Ke's magic weakened and he returned to his lizard form, but every day, in the form of a man, Toc Ke visited the girl in her village. He brought her the sweetest fruit and took her for long walks. He recited poetry and braided flowers into her long, dark hair. Soon, the girl fell in love with Toc Ke and agreed to marry him. Toc Ke was happy, but he was also sad because he was afraid she would leave him if she ever discovered his secret. And so he told her that he had to work deep in the forest at night and could be with her only in the daytime. Because she loved him, she agreed to this arrangement.

By day, Toc Ke worked as a man to build a house for his bride-to-be, but at night he disappeared into the forest as a lizard, leaving the girl with her family. When the house was finished, Toc Ke married the girl, and on their wedding day, they held a feast. The happy couple danced for hours, but when the sun began to set, Toc Ke knew that he needed to get to the forest quickly.

Toc Ke scooped up his bride and raced across the field to their new home, but when they got there, she begged him not to leave. *How could he abandon her on their wedding night?* he thought. So he struggled with his magic, fighting to keep his human form for just a little longer. Time went quickly, and Toc Ke's bride began to fall asleep—but not before she saw Toc Ke turn back into a lizard. She cried out.

Toc Ke, believing he had ruined everything, scurried into the forest. But his bride chased after him, calling his name, "Toc Ke! Toc Ke!"

Toc Ke couldn't believe it. *Did she truly love him?* he wondered. He turned back and met his bride in the darkness. "Yes," she told him, "it's true love." He blushed deeply, and orange spots covered his skin. "You look so handsome!" his bride exclaimed. And to prove her devotion, she asked him to turn her into a spotted lizard just like him. That way, she promised, they could be together forever. To this day, you can hear her call his name in the dark forest: *Toc Ke! Toc Ke!*

GLOSSARY

camouflage – the ability to hide, due to coloring or markings that blend in with a given environment

captive-bred – having been bred and raised in a place from which escape is not possible

colonized – established settlements in a new land and exercised rule over them

cultures – particular groups in a society that share behaviors and characteristics that are accepted as normal by that group

ecosystem – a community of organisms that live together in an environment

embryos – unborn or unhatched offspring in the early stages of development

extinction – the act or process of becoming extinct; coming to an end or dying out

genetic – relating to genes, the basic physical units of heredity

gravid – carrying fertilized eggs or unborn offspring inside the body

membranes – thin, clear layers of tissue that cover an internal organ or developing organism

molecules – the smallest units of chemical matter that make up everything in the universe

morphologist – a scientist who studies the form and properties of living organisms

mythology – a collection of myths, or popular, traditional beliefs or stories that explain how something came to be or that are associated with a person or object

parasites – animals or plants that live on or inside another living thing (called a host) while giving nothing back to the host; some parasites cause disease or even death

physicist – a scientist who studies the properties of matter and energy

SELECTED BIBLIOGRAPHY

ARKive. "Lined Day Gecko (*Phelsuma lineata*)." http://www.arkive.org/lined-day-gecko/phelsuma-lineata/.

Badger, David. *Lizards: A Natural History of Some Uncommon Creatures—Extraordinary Chameleons, Iguanas, Geckos, & More*. Stillwater, Minn.: Voyageur Press, 2002.

BBC. "Science & Nature: Wildfacts; Tokay Gecko." http://www.bbc.co.uk/nature/wildfacts/factfiles/476.shtml.

Forbes, Peter. *The Gecko's Foot: How Scientists are Taking a Leaf from Nature's Book*. New York: Harper Perennial, 2011.

Mattison, Chris. *Firefly Encyclopedia of Reptiles and Amphibians*. 2nd ed. Buffalo, N.Y.: Firefly Books, 2008.

Smithsonian National Zoological Park. "Fact Sheets: Madagascar Giant Day Gecko." http://nationalzoo.si.edu/Animals/ReptilesAmphibians/Facts/FactSheets/Madagascargiantdaygecko.cfm.

Note: Every effort has been made to ensure that any websites listed above were active at the time of publication. However, because of the nature of the Internet, it is impossible to guarantee that these sites will remain active indefinitely or that their contents will not be altered.

One year after New Caledonian crested geckos were declared extinct in 1993, they were rediscovered.

INDEX